ANCIENT
CHINA
INSIDE OUT

Kelly Spence

Crabtree Publishing Company
www.crabtreebooks.com

ANCIENT WORLDS INSIDE OUT

Author: Kelly Spence

Editors: Sarah Eason, Kelly Spence, Janine Deschenes, and Kathy Middleton

Editorial director: Kathy Middleton

Design: Paul Myerscough

Cover design: Paul Myerscough

Photo research: Rachel Blount

Proofreader: Wendy Scavuzzo

Production coordinator and Prepress technician: Tammy McGarr

Print coordinator: Margaret Amy Salter

Consultant: John Malam, archaeologist

Written and produced for Crabtree Publishing Company by Calcium Creative

Front Cover
BKGD: The Great Wall built by China's first emperor Qin Shihuangdi during the 3rd century BCE.
Inset: A terracotta soldier, one of more than 8,000 sculptures that make up the Terracotta Army buried with the first emperor of China.
Title Page
BKGD: The curvy roads of the Silk Route, an ancient trading route that stretched from China to Europe.
Inset: A Han Dynasty terracotta sculpture of a servant from 206 BCE.

Photo Credits:

t=Top, bl=Bottom Left, br=Bottom Right

Alamy: ZUMA Press, Inc.: p. 16–17; Getty Images: DEA/G. DAGLI ORTI/Contributor: p. 21b; Zhang Peng/LightRocket: p. 28b;

LACMA www.lacma.org: Gift of Mr. and Mrs. Eric Lidow: p. 17b, p. 23t;

Shutterstock: Aphotostory: p. 22–23; Cl2004lhy: p. 11t; Chen WS: p. 28–29; Contax66: p. 18–19; Pius Lee: p. 8–9; Giancarlo Liguori: p. 10–11; Stephen Marques: p. 5c; Rudra Narayan Mitra: p. 1bg, p. 24–25; Sihasakprachum: p. 27b; Alexander Vershinin: p. 6–7; Mo Wu: p. 4–5; The Walters Art Museum: Acquired by Henry Walters, 1920: p. 19t; Museum purchase, 1949: p. 25b; Wikimedia Commons: BabelStone: p. 15t; Guillaume Jacquet: p. 1fg, p. 13br; Wang Jie: p. 3, p. 14–15; Rolfmueller: p. 12–13; Wit: p. 26–27; Zhao 1974: p. 20–21.

Map p. 5 by Geoff Ward. Artwork p. 29 by Venetia Dean.

Cover: Shutterstock: Hung Chung Chih (br), Sean Pavone (bg)

Library and Archives Canada Cataloguing in Publication

Spence, Kelly, author
    Ancient China inside out / Kelly Spence.

(Ancient worlds inside out)
Includes index.
Issued in print and electronic formats.
ISBN 978-0-7787-2868-9 (hardcover).--
ISBN 978-0-7787-2875-7 (softcover).--
ISBN 978-1-4271-1845-5 (HTML)

    1. China--Social life and customs--To 221 B.C.--Juvenile literature. 2. China--Civilization--To 221 B.C.--Juvenile literature. 3. China--Antiquities--Juvenile literature. 4. Material culture--China--Juvenile literature. 5. China--History--To 221 B.C.--Juvenile literature. I. Title.

DS741.65.S64 2017   j931   C2016-907255-X
                                          C2016-907256-8

Library of Congress Cataloging-in-Publication Data

Names: Spence, Kelly, author.
Title: Ancient China inside out / Kelly Spence.
Description: New York, New York : Crabtree Publishing Company, 2017. | Series: Ancient worlds inside out | Includes index.
Identifiers: LCCN 2017000078 (print) | LCCN 2017004860 (ebook) | ISBN 9780778728689 (reinforced library binding : alkaline paper) | ISBN 9780778728757 (paperback : alkaline paper) | ISBN 9781427118455 (Electronic HTML)
Subjects: LCSH: China--Civilization--To 221 B.C.--Juvenile literature. | China--Civilization--221 B.C.-960 A.D.--Juvenile literature.
Classification: LCC DS741.65 .S69 2017 (print) | LCC DS741.65 (ebook) | DDC 931--dc23
LC record available at https://lccn.loc.gov/2017000078

Crabtree Publishing Company

www.crabtreebooks.com   1-800-387-7650

Printed in Canada/032017/EF20170202

Copyright © **2017 CRABTREE PUBLISHING COMPANY**. All rights reserved. No part of this publication may be reproduced, stored in a retrieval system or be transmitted in any form or by any means, electronic, mechanical, photocopying, recording, or otherwise, without the prior written permission of Crabtree Publishing Company. In Canada: We acknowledge the financial support of the Government of Canada through the Canada Book Fund for our publishing activities.

Published in Canada
Crabtree Publishing
616 Welland Ave.
St. Catharines, Ontario
L2M 5V6

Published in the United States
Crabtree Publishing
PMB 59051
350 Fifth Avenue, 59th Floor
New York, New York 10118

Published in the United Kingdom
Crabtree Publishing
Maritime House
Basin Road North, Hove
BN41 1WR

Published in Australia
Crabtree Publishing
3 Charles Street
Coburg North
VIC, 3058

CONTENTS

WHO WERE THE ANCIENT CHINESE?

For more than 4,000 years, people have called the lands that make up present-day China home. One of the world's oldest civilizations, ancient China developed from early settlements along the banks of the Yangtze River and the Yellow River. It became a land of innovation and invention.

Rivers, Mountains, and Deserts

The geography of China helped shape its civilization. The mighty Himalaya Mountains rise to the south of China, and the Taklamakan Desert and Gobi Desert stretch along its northern and western borders. These towering peaks and dry deserts created a natural barrier that **isolated** the ancient Chinese from their neighbors. Winding across China from west to east are the Yangtze River and Yellow River. It was along the **fertile** banks of those two waterways that the first settlements sprung up, around 3500 B.C.E.

A United Kingdom

For hundreds of years, China was divided into several small **kingdoms**. Each kingdom was ruled by a **dynasty**, or a line of rulers from a single family. The Shang Dynasty (1600–1046 B.C.E.) and the Zhou Dynasty (1046–256 B.C.E.) were two powerful kingdoms that controlled large parts of ancient China. In 221 B.C.E., several small kingdoms were joined together as a single **empire** under the first emperor, Shihuangdi. This was called the Qin Dynasty.

Trade and Innovation

The ancient Chinese learned how to create a luxurious fabric from the **cocoons** of silkworms. Called silk, this fabric was transported along an extensive **trade** route that ran west to the Mediterranean Sea, linking ancient China to other early civilizations. Because of the importance of silk as a trade good, the route was known as the Silk Road. Other Chinese inventions include paper, printing, the compass, and gunpowder.

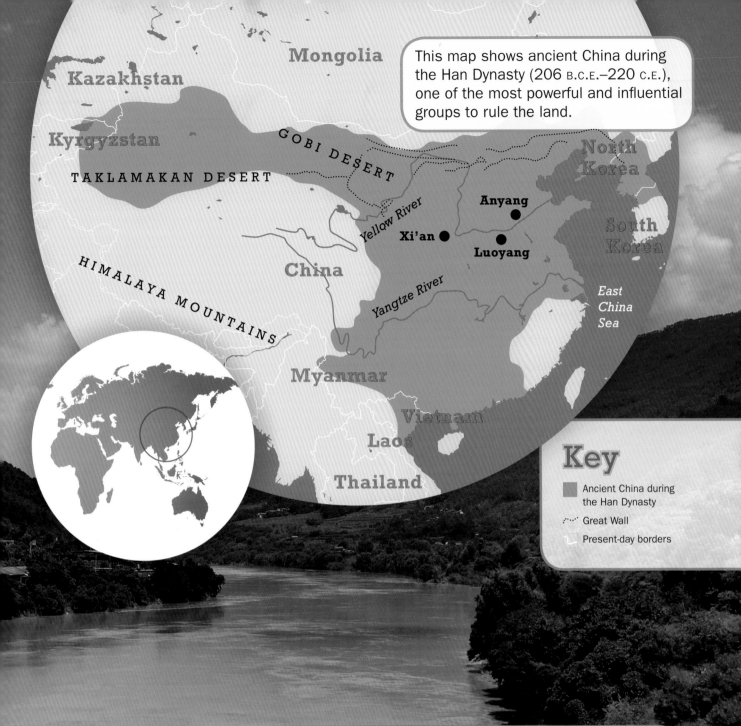

This map shows ancient China during the Han Dynasty (206 B.C.E.–220 C.E.), one of the most powerful and influential groups to rule the land.

Mongolia

Kazakhstan

Kyrgyzstan

GOBI DESERT

TAKLAMAKAN DESERT

North Korea

Yellow River

Anyang

Xi'an

Luoyang

South Korea

HIMALAYA MOUNTAINS

China

Yangtze River

East China Sea

Myanmar

Vietnam

Laos

Thailand

Key

Ancient China during the Han Dynasty

Great Wall

Present-day borders

The Yellow River, called the Huang He by the Chinese, is 3,395 miles (5,464 km) long. The waterway is named for its yellow color, caused by a yellow dust called loess that blows into it.

What Is an Ancient Civilization?

Large settlements of people formed the basis of the first civilizations. Through practices such as farming and the development of writing systems, government, and class systems, the settlements of people grew into large cities. These ancient civilizations led to the later development of present-day cities, states, and countries.

DIGGING UP THE PAST

In 1974, while digging a well in northwest China, farmers discovered pieces of a life-size figure. An **excavation** of the site by an archaeological team led to the discovery of thousands of **terra-cotta** warriors, which were created to guard the tomb, or burial chamber, of Emperor Shihuangdi. Uncovering the terra-cotta warriors marked the most significant archaeological find from ancient China—so far.

Living Forever

Some of the best-preserved **artifacts** from ancient China have been discovered in tombs. People were buried in tombs with small objects called *mingqi*. The ancient Chinese believed that the dead would need these objects in the **afterlife**. They included miniature models of houses, **granaries**, entertainers, servants, and food.

The Lost Dynasty

The first dynasty to rule ancient China was the Xia Dynasty. There is still much to be learned about it. Estimated to have existed around 2070 to 1600 B.C.E., the Xia was ruled by Yu, who is known as the Yellow Emperor. He is famous for building **canals** to control the annual flooding of the Yellow River. When Yu passed down power to his son, beginning the familial line of rulers, the first dynasty began. Although information about the Xia Dynasty was recorded by later dynasties, no written materials created by the Xia Dynasty have been discovered to confirm its existence. Some archaeologists believe that **Neolithic** artifacts such as pottery may have been made during the Xia Dynasty. Other experts think that the dynasty is only a **legend**.

More than 6,000 terra-cotta warriors have been unearthed in the city of Xi'an, close to the burial mound of Shihuangdi.

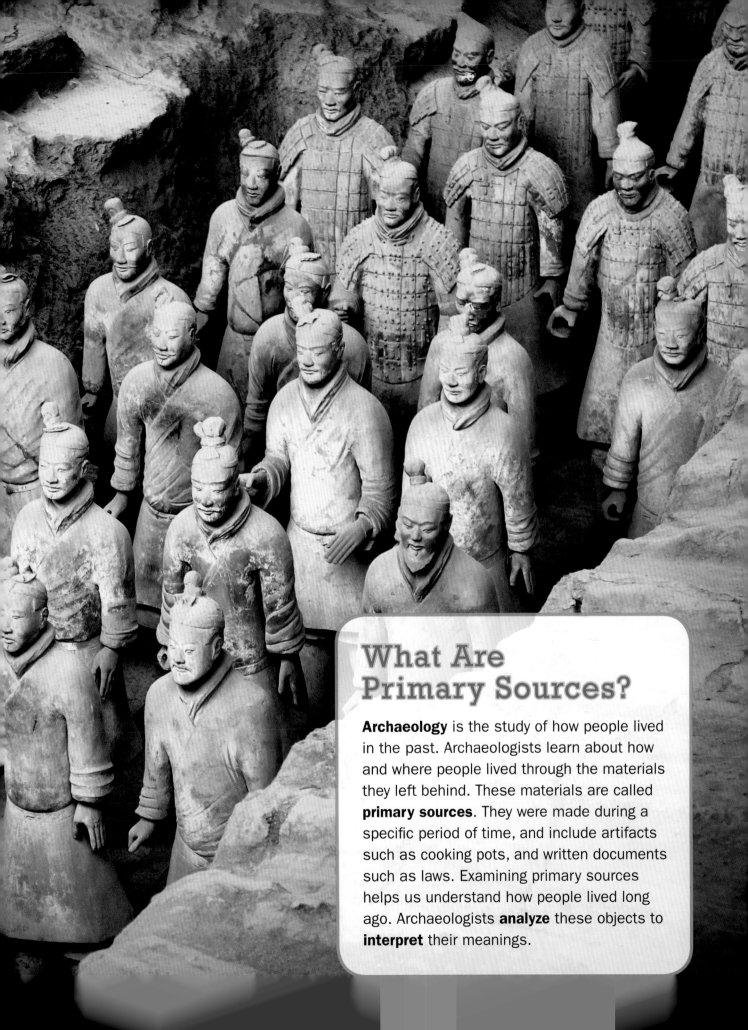

What Are Primary Sources?

Archaeology is the study of how people lived in the past. Archaeologists learn about how and where people lived through the materials they left behind. These materials are called **primary sources**. They were made during a specific period of time, and include artifacts such as cooking pots, and written documents such as laws. Examining primary sources helps us understand how people lived long ago. Archaeologists **analyze** these objects to **interpret** their meanings.

FOOD AND FARMING

The rich soil along the banks of the Yellow and Yangtze rivers was ideal for farming. In the north, along the banks of the Yellow River, a grain called millet was grown. Farther south, near the Yangtze River, rice was the most important crop.

Terraces of Rice

Much of China is covered in rolling hills. To grow crops on sloped land, the people cut long, flat **terraces** like steps into the sides of mountains. The terraces were flooded with water to help rice grow. Two or three crops could be harvested in a single year. Other important crops included millet, wheat, and barley.

Working the Land

The wheelbarrow was invented in China. It allowed people to easily transport heavy loads. The ancient Chinese also raised animals, including cattle, horses, pigs, chickens, and dogs, to use for labor. The plow was invented to turn the soil, and a seed drill sped up the process of planting seeds in the ground. Each of these inventions helped farmers provide food for the growing population of the empire.

Irrigation

In 256 B.C.E., construction began on an **irrigation** system intended to control the annual flooding of the Min River, which flows into the Yangtze. A **levee** was built to carry the extra water away. More than 2,000 years later, the system, known as the Dujiangyan irrigation system after the city it is located near, continues to carry water to farmland in Sichuan province in southwest China.

Curving terraces of rice form the Dragon's Backbone, a collection of terraces on Longji Mountain. These terraces have been used to grow rice since the Yuan Dynasty.

trip-hammer

History Up Close

Grains of rice are protected in hard, thick coverings called husks. The grains must be pounded to remove the husk. This was first accomplished in ancient China by using a **mortar** and **pestle**, which later evolved into the trip-hammer. This miniature terra-cotta model of a trip-hammer dates from the 1st to the 3rd century c.e., during the Eastern Han period. It was discovered in a tomb.

A trip-hammer worked like a seesaw. The user stepped down on the raised arm, which lifted the large stone attached to the other end. Grains of rice were placed in the hollowed section beneath the stone, then the arm was released. The blow from the heavy stone cracked the husks. Tools such as this were much less labor intensive and could produce larger volumes of husked grains. After the grains were pounded, air was blown over them to remove the broken husks. Some may have been ground more to make flour.

EMPERORS AND DYNASTIES

Ancient Chinese history is divided into time periods by dynasties—periods of time during which a line of rulers from a single family controlled the land. Power was passed down from one generation to the next. Dynastic rule continued in China until 1912.

The First Dynasties

The Shang Dynasty is traditionally dated from 1766 to 1122 B.C.E. Shang rulers were the first to record history and had several **capitals**, the last at Anyang. The Shang Dynasty was overthrown by the Zhou, who ruled a region to the west. During the Zhou Dynasty, the kingdom was divided into several territories that were ruled by the king's relatives.

The Mandate of Heaven

Beginning during the Zhou Dynasty, the emperor's rule was **justified** under a principle, or belief, called the Mandate of Heaven. The mandate set out that a ruler was given the right to rule by *tian*, or heaven. As the "son of heaven," the emperor had to be a just and **moral** leader. Many dynasties were overthrown once another group determined that the current emperor was no longer following the Mandate of Heaven.

United as One

In 221 B.C.E., Shihuangdi seized power and united several warring states into one powerful empire. Although Shihuangdi's rule did not last long, China remained unified as a single empire for thousands of years. The Qin Dynasty, first ruled by Shihuangdi, was followed by the Han (206 B.C.E. to 220 C.E.), the Six Dynasties period (220 to 589 C.E.), Sui (581 to 618 C.E.), Tang (618 to 907 C.E.), Five Dynasties period (907 to 960 C.E.), Song (960 to 1279 C.E.), Yuan (1279 to 1368 C.E.), Ming (1368 to 1644 C.E.), and Qing (1644 to 1911 C.E.) dynasties.

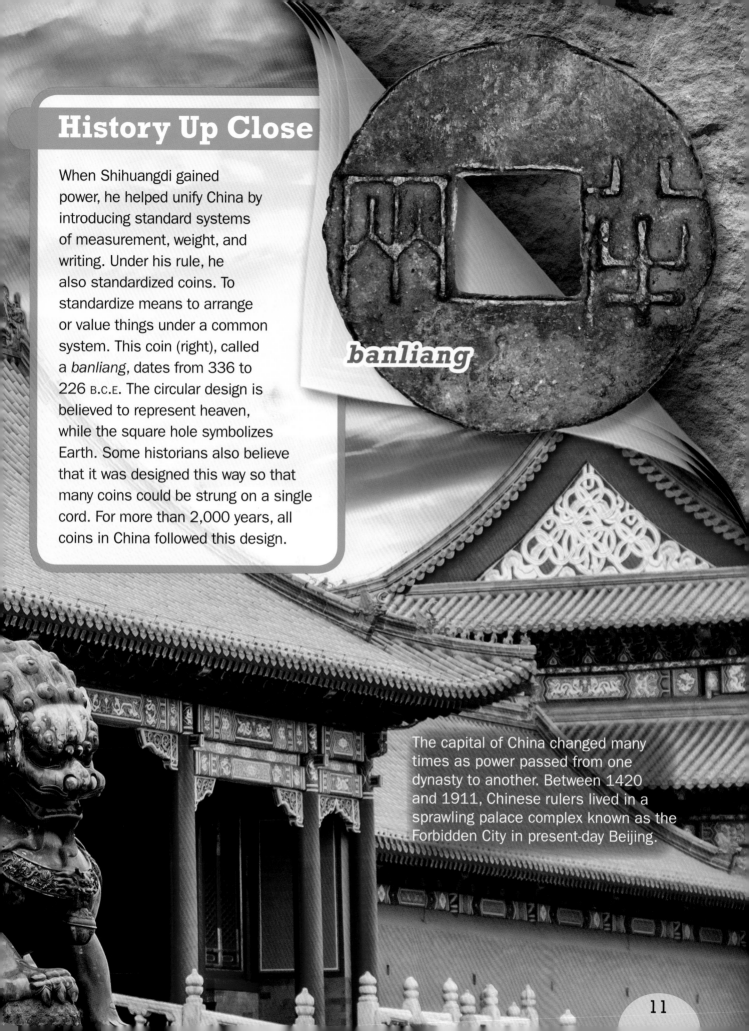

History Up Close

When Shihuangdi gained power, he helped unify China by introducing standard systems of measurement, weight, and writing. Under his rule, he also standardized coins. To standardize means to arrange or value things under a common system. This coin (right), called a *banliang*, dates from 336 to 226 B.C.E. The circular design is believed to represent heaven, while the square hole symbolizes Earth. Some historians also believe that it was designed this way so that many coins could be strung on a single cord. For more than 2,000 years, all coins in China followed this design.

banliang

The capital of China changed many times as power passed from one dynasty to another. Between 1420 and 1911, Chinese rulers lived in a sprawling palace complex known as the Forbidden City in present-day Beijing.

11

EVERYDAY LIFE

The majority of people in ancient China were farmers. They harvested the immense amounts of food needed to feed the growing population. During the Han Dynasty, the population of China swelled from about 60 million to 150 million.

Four Classes of People

Around the 4th century B.C.E., ancient texts reveal that Chinese society was divided into four classes. Members of the educated class, who worked as **scholars** and political leaders, were known as the *shi*. Farmers, called the *nong*, were highly respected because they grew the food that fed the large population. The *gong* were craftspeople, who made items such as pottery, and the *shang* were traders and merchants. Above these four classes, the emperor ruled with absolute power. Below were the servants and slaves.

Family Life

Men were much more powerful than women in ancient Chinese society, so the birth of a son was celebrated far more than that of a daughter. In the *Liji*, or *Book of Records*, parents were instructed to teach their children in different ways. According to the book, boys were taught to respond clearly and boldly when spoken to; while girls should speak in a low and **submissive** way. Boys born into noble families were sent to school, but girls remained at home until they married. They were taught how to cook, clean, and practice the art of silk making. Families in ancient China lived together under one roof— sometimes for many generations. Great respect was shown to elders and the ancestors. The ancient Chinese believed that their relatives continued to watch over the family as spirits. By making sacrifices to their ancestors, they would receive good fortune. Most households included a shrine—an area where offerings were placed for the ancestors.

This model shows the ancient city of Linzi in eastern China. During the 4th and 3rd centuries B.C.E., an estimated 350,000 people lived in the city.

History Up Close

The nobility made many preparations for the afterlife. During the Shang and Zhou dynasties, a ruler's attendants were killed and buried with their masters so they could continue to serve them in the next life. By the Han Dynasty, small symbolic figures were placed in tombs instead. This terra-cotta statue of a servant girl dates from 206 B.C.E. to 9 C.E., during the Western Han period. It was found in a tomb in northern China.

servant statue

Dig Deeper!

Why do you think ancient Chinese society was divided into four social classes? What might some benefits of this system include? Explain your reasoning.

READING AND WRITING

The first Chinese characters, or written marks, were **pictograms**, which are small drawings that represent words and ideas. According to legend, Cangjie, the inventor of Chinese writing, drew inspiration for the pictograms from the scratch marks left by animals and by the shape of landforms such as mountains.

Paper and Printing

Early Chinese texts were written on silk and wood. The invention of paper was first recorded during the Han Dynasty in 105 C.E. Paper was created by soaking small pieces of plant fiber, such as mulberry bark, bamboo, and hemp, in water. Called pulp, the substance was spread in an even layer and left to dry. A substance inside the fibers caused the dried pulp to bind together as a single sheet. With the invention of paper, it became much easier and less costly for texts to be produced on a larger scale by printing, which was another Chinese invention. During the Tang Dynasty, blocks of wood were carved with Buddhist scriptures, then coated with ink and stamped on various materials.

Inspired by Nature

Like many Chinese art forms, **calligraphy** and painting were inspired by nature. For both painters and calligraphers, their important tools were ink, a brush, an inkstone, and paper. Fashioned out of stone or another hard material, an inkstone was used to prepare ink. A stick of ink was dipped into water, then ground along the rough surface of the stone. A brush was dipped into the ink and used to create the smooth strokes of a written character or the flowing lines of a painting.

Called the *Diamond Sutra*, the world's oldest book bearing a date was printed in ancient China in 868 C.E. The book was discovered in the Dunhuang Caves, which is a sacred Buddhist site.

oracle bone

History Up Close

This oracle bone dates from around 1200 B.C.E. and was discovered at Anyang, the last capital of the Shang Dynasty. Bones such as this were used for **divination** by the Shang and Zhou. After the bones were cleaned, small holes were cut into the smooth surface. A fortune-teller wrote a question on the bone, as well as two answers—one positive and one negative. The holes were heated until the bone cracked. The cracks were interpreted to answer the question. The answer, as well as the date of the reading, was often recorded on the bone.

Dig Deeper!

As time passed, rulers themselves began interpreting the cracks on oracle bones. Why might a ruler want to read the cracks in the bone himself? Explain your reasoning.

SKILLED CRAFTSPEOPLE

Pottery and objects fashioned from jade and bronze reveal the high level of craftsmanship mastered by the Chinese. Their work eventually marked the beginning of the Bronze Age, around 1700 B.C.E.

The Power of Jade

Many artifacts from ancient China were carved from a hard green stone called jade. A rough paste made with sand was used to wear away and shape the hard stone. Other tools were used to make holes. A finer sand was used to polish the finished piece. Jade burial suits were popular among the Han nobility. To make a suit, squares or rectangles of jade were stitched together using thread. The color of the thread was determined by a person's position. Gold thread was reserved for the emperor, and silver and copper were used for members of the nobility. Jade was more highly prized than gold, and was believed to hold mystical powers. Before full suits were created, small jade plugs were placed over the body's holes, such as the eyes and nostrils, to protect the body from evil spirits. By the end of the Han rule, jade burial suits were outlawed. It took a lot of time to make them, and they became viewed as too elaborate.

Built to Last

Bronze was a longer-lasting and more affordable material. Copper, tin, and lead were heated, then melted and shaped into clay molds to make weapons and tools, cups, bowls, and cookware. Today, many bronze artifacts are green, however, when they were made they would have appeared golden brown. Large foundries, or workshops where metal is melted and shaped, were common in northern areas. **Ceramics** could be crafted on a potter's wheel, or created by coiling long ropes of clay. They were then fired to harden at a high temperature in a special oven, called a kiln.

The ruins of a dragon kiln were unearthed in Nanning in southern China. Many ceramic objects could be fired at one time inside this long kiln in chambers that rose up over several steps, resembling the ridges on a dragon's back.

History Up Close

This bronze bell, called a *zhong*, was made around 850 to 771 B.C.E., during the Zhou Dynasty. A cord would have been passed through the hole on top to hold the bell on an angle. The bell is not rung by a **clapper** inside. Instead, it is struck with a wooden hammer. The **elliptical** shape of the bottom allows the bell to produce two different sounds, depending on where it is hit. Thousands of years ago, the ringing of the bell might have signaled for soldiers to retreat during battle, or carried a message to a person's ancestors. Large sets of bells were also played for entertainment.

zhong

17

THE THREE WAYS

For thousands or years, three important belief systems—Buddhism, Daoism, and Confucianism—peacefully existed in China during the same period. Together, these religions became known as "The Three Ways."

Buddhism

Buddhism started in the 5th century B.C.E. It arrived in China during the Han Dynasty, carried along the Silk Road from India. The goal of Buddhism is to achieve enlightenment, which means to achieve spiritual awakening. Followers believe in rebirth after death, and that this cycle can only reach completion after a person has lived a good, moral life. During the Tang era, Buddhism became especially popular in China, with many men becoming **monks**.

Daoism

Dao means "way." Daoism was founded in China by Laozi, a scholar of the Zhou Dynasty. Daoism promotes living a simple life, in balance and harmony with the natural world. A well-known symbol of Daoism is the yin and yang, in which positive and negative forces are balanced.

Confucianism

Confucianism, also beginning in China, is named after Confucius—a **philosopher** who taught about morals, family, and the importance of a strong government. During the Han Dynasty, this was the dominant religion in ancient China. Confucian texts were used for the government exams and studied in most schools.

Buddha is the founder of Buddhism. The Leshan Buddha is the largest carving of Buddha in the world. It stands 233 feet (71 m) tall.

History Up Close

This small wooden shrine dates from the Song Dynasty (960–1279 C.E.). It is only 7.5 inches (19 cm) tall, yet is remarkably detailed. Buddha sits cross-legged in the center. A **pagoda** is shown above his head. In Buddhism, a pagoda indicates the Lotus sutra, or scripture, which is one of the key texts of the faith. The sutra states that everyone has the potential within themselves for enlightenment.

Two **bodhisattvas**, or individuals who have achieved enlightenment, appear on the top of each outer panel. One rides an elephant and the other sits on a lion. The shrine was carved from a single piece of wood and could be folded shut. Shrines such as this were carried by monks as they spread the Buddhist faith throughout China and the rest of Asia.

shrine

Dig Deeper!

How might the positions of the figures in the shrine draw people to Buddhism? Explain your reasoning.

ENGINEERING AND STRUCTURES

Many of the structures of ancient China were built of wood and bamboo. Over thousands of years, these structures have rotted away. However, the small ceramic models of houses, watchtowers, granaries, and other structures left in tombs provide a wealth of information.

Stone by Stone

The ancient Chinese were skilled builders. Some bridges they built from stone remain in use today, thousands of years after they were constructed. Many were designed with arches to support the weight of the stones. Other bridges were built by attaching wooden planks to cables that were made by weaving together strips of bamboo.

Tombs

After burial, a ruler's tomb was covered with wood and earth to form a mound. Temples were built nearby so that people could leave offerings for their ancestors. Inside the tombs, there were several chambers, filled with objects needed for the afterlife, as well as the ruler's body. In Xi'an, the burial mound of Emperor Shihuangdi has lain untouched for more than 2,000 years. Records tell of a life-size kingdom inside the tomb, surrounded by rivers of **mercury**, a poisonous metal. Archaeologists have tested the soil around the mound and discovered high levels of mercury, suggesting that these ancient sources are correct.

The Grand Canal

During the Sui Dynasty, Emperor Yan wanted to connect China's waterways from north to south. He ordered the construction of a canal, or human-made waterway, to transport rice grown in the south to the people in the north. Over thousands of years, the canal was expanded. Today, the canal stretches 1,104 miles (1,776 km) across China. The Grand Canal is still in use today and is the world's oldest canal.

History Up Close

Small models of buildings were placed in tombs as *mingqi*. This three-story ceramic watchtower dates from the 1st to 3rd century C.E. Two figures armed with crossbows appear on the second level. From their perch, they could spot approaching enemies from a distance. This tower may have been placed in a tomb to protect a deceased person in the afterlife. Some archaeologists believe that the curved design of the tiled roof was to repel evil spirits that traveled in straight lines. It also served a practical purpose by directing rain and snow away from the structure, and letting in lots of sunlight.

watchtower

The Zhaozhou Bridge was built entirely of stone during the Sui Dynasty. It is the oldest standing bridge in China.

MILITARY AND DEFENSE

The kingdoms of ancient China were often at war with one another. Even after the country was unified into one empire, enemies from neighboring lands remained a threat.

The Great Wall of China

In 221 B.C.E., Emperor Shihuangdi ordered that existing walls built by earlier kingdoms were to be linked together in the north to protect his newly united kingdom. It is estimated that 700,000 people worked on constructing the wall. In places, the wall was made from **rammed earth**, while in other places stone and wood were used. Towers and gates were built at certain points to allow passage through the wall. If a section of the wall came under attack, soldiers at the nearest tower lit fires to alert others at towers farther along the wall.

Strong Weapons

Gun powder was first discovered by scientists who were searching for a recipe for **immortality**. While the powder did not deliver eternal life, it was extremely effective in battle. Gunpowder was stuffed into bamboo tubes that were filled with pieces of iron—a type of metal. When lit, the gunpowder exploded, launching the pieces of iron at the enemy. The crossbow was also invented in China. This weapon consists of a short bow mounted across a wooden block. When the bow is pulled back and released, it fires short arrows. Crossbows were used in combat by the 5th century B.C.E.

Under Mongol Rule

In 1211, the Mongols—**barbarians** from the north—invaded China to gain control of more territory. The two groups fought for many years, but the Mongols had a stronger army. Their leader Kublai Khan started the Yuan Dynasty in 1279. The Mongols were driven out of China by the Ming Dynasty in 1368.

ge

The Great Wall of China winds 5,500 miles (8,850 km) across the Chinese countryside.

History Up Close

During the Shang Dynasty, the ancient Chinese began using weapons called *ge* in warfare. This blade is all that remains from this weapon, because the wooden handle rotted away centuries ago. This blade is 8 inches (21 cm) long, and dates from 1300–1050 B.C.E. It was likely found in the province of Henan, near the Shang capital of Anyang. A pig is etched into the piece that would have been attached to the handle. These dagger-axes provided a deadly blow. When swung, the sharp blade could slice through armor. By the Han Dynasty, *ge* were not as commonly used. The spear proved more effective in battle.

TRADE AND TRAVEL

The Silk Road was an extensive network of land and water routes that linked many great civilizations together. Luxurious silk, finely crafted ceramics, and exotic spices and flowers were carried west from China to faraway lands. Goods such as gold, glass, perfume, and wool were brought east to China along these winding roads. Along with these goods also came religions, technologies, and much more.

The Secret of Silk

The Silk Road was named for the luxurious fabric the Chinese invented. This soft, lightweight fabric is made from the cocoons of silkworms. The soft cocoons are harvested, then boiled to loosen the fibers. Fibers are thread-like materials, which can be unraveled into individual threads. During the Tang Dynasty, about 30 percent of Chinese trade was made up of silk. Chinese silks dating from the Han Dynasty have been discovered in faraway places, such as Egypt and Rome. The secret of silk-making was closely guarded for hundreds of years. It was even punishable by death to take silkworms out of China. But the secret was eventually discovered by other ancient civilizations.

Routes by Sea

The ancient Chinese were also skilled sailors. A junk was a sailing vessel with a flat, wide bottom. A flat piece of wood, called a rudder, was first used by the Chinese to steer the boat on a straight course. The Chinese were superstitious; an eye was painted on each side of the **stern** so the ship could see where it was going. By the early Middle Ages, the Chinese had sailed in junks to waters near present-day Indonesia and India. The great seaman Zheng He (1371–1433 c.e.) led seven voyages during the Ming Dynasty. His voyages helped extend Chinese control over other parts of Southeast Asia.

The Silk Road began in Xi'an in northwest China, and stretched more than 4,000 miles (6,437 km).

History Up Close

This figure of a camel dates from the Tang Dynasty (618–907 C.E.). It was formed from clay using a mold, then covered in a colorful glaze, or glossy coating. Camels were used to carry goods along trade routes because they could travel vast distances across the dry desert with little water. Historians believe that statues of camels symbolized the wealth that trade brought to ancient China. Many have been found in tombs. This may reflect a belief that these animals carried goods for the deceased into the afterlife. It also may have symbolized the wealth the deceased person gained during their life through trade along the Silk Road.

camel statue

ENDURING CHINA

While many other great civilizations came to an end, China carried on. Its legacy continues today, with many of its traditions and landmarks rooted in the country's rich past. The Qing Dynasty, the last to rule China, was overthrown in 1911, when the country became a **republic**.

A Golden Age

Although the Chinese have recorded history for centuries, it is only within the last 100 years that some of the most exciting archaeological discoveries have been made. The Chinese government is working to uncover new sites, while also preserving the sites and artifacts that have already been uncovered. The Great Wall is perhaps the most recognizable symbol of China, and helps to link the country's past to its present. During different periods, the wall has been added to and repaired. Today, much work is being done to preserve this important link to China's past.

The Story Continues

Archaeologists continue to make discoveries that reveal new information about China's rich history. Sometimes, new findings completely change our understanding of the past. In 2016, archaeologists studying the terra-cotta warriors suggested that their lifelike design was inspired by Greek statues, and that Greek sculptors may have worked on the army in China. DNA evidence supports the theory that Europeans were in China. This reveals a connection between the two great civilizations more than 1,500 years before the Italian explorer Marco Polo reached China during the late 1200s. The question of how, and when, these two civilizations first encountered one another is another puzzle for archaeologists to solve.

The construction of the burial mound of Shihuangdi began in 246 B.C.E. More than 2,000 years later, the wonders hidden within the burial mound continue to fascinate archaeologists.

History Up Close

The terra-cotta warriors date from around 221 B.C.E., when Emperor Shihuangdi first ordered the building of his tomb complex in Xi'an. Each soldier has unique facial features, right down to their ears. While the discovery of the tomb complex has revealed a wealth of information about Emperor Shihuangdi, the terra-cotta army continues to guard many secrets of the first emperor's tomb.

terra-cotta warrior

WHICH WAY TO GO?

The compass, which is a tool used for navigation, was invented in ancient China. The first compasses were used for divination, or to try to predict the future. They were later used as a practical tool by ancient Chinese sailors.

Finding the Way

During the day, ancient Chinese sailors navigated by the position of the Sun in the sky. At night or on cloudy days, a "south-pointer" could be used to figure out which way was north or south. Records from the late Song Dynasty tell of a compass called a "south-pointer" that was made by rubbing a needle against a substance that was naturally magnetic, such as a **lodestone**. The needle became temporarily magnetized and aligned to Earth's poles, which indicate the directions of north and south. When attached to cork or wood and floated in water or hung from a string, the needle pointed north–south.

This "south-pointer" was discovered in a shipwreck near Quanzhou, which was an important trading port during the Song Dynasty.

Activity:

Make a Chinese Water Compass!

Find your way like the ancient Chinese!

You Will Need:

- Cork
- Utility knife
- Needle
- Magnet
- Paper clip
- Small dish
- Water
- Adult supervision

Instructions

1. Fill the small dish halfway with water.
2. With an adult's help, use the utility knife to cut the cork in half.
3. Rub the magnet along the needle only from top to bottom in even strokes. After a minute or two, hold the needle near a paper clip to test whether it is magnetized.
4. Once the needle is ready, ask an adult to help you carefully push it through the cork. Place the cork in the water. Set the dish in the center of a table and make sure there is no metal nearby. The needle will swing to point north–south.

The Challenge

Think about how you could make a waterproof lid for your compass to make it portable. For example, you could use plastic wrap for a see-through lid, and a rubber band or tape to secure the lid. Once you have designed and made your lid, try out your compass while on the move! Ask an adult to drive you in a car while you hold your compass. Take a modern compass with you, too. Do the movements of your water compass match those of your modern compass? How effective is the water compass as a navigation system?

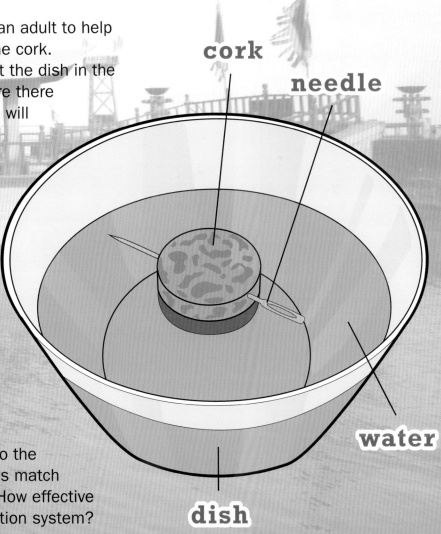

cork

needle

water

dish

GLOSSARY

Note: Some bold-faced words are defined where they appear in the text.

afterlife Life after death

analyze To examine

artifacts Objects made by humans that date from a certain period of time

barbarians Uncivilized people

bodhisattvas In Buddhism, individuals who achieve enlightenment and help others to do the same

calligraphy Decorative handwriting

canals Waterways built by humans, and used for travel and to drain and irrigate land

capital The most important city or town in a country or region; it is usually where the government is located and is the place from where the country or region is controlled

ceramics Objects made from clay that are hardened by baking

clapper The tongue inside a bell that allows it to ring

cocoons Cases spun by insect larvae, or non-adult insects, to protect their bodies as they change and grow

divination Using magic to predict the future

elliptical Oval or egg-shaped

empire A large area with several territories under the control of a single ruler called an emperor

excavation The process of digging something up

fertile Able to produce lots of vegetation, such as fruits, grains, and vegetables

granaries Buildings used to store grains

immortality The ability to live forever

interpret To figure out the meaning

irrigation A process in which water is carried somewhere to water crops or land, usually by human-made canals or other technologies

isolated Separated from others

jade A hard green stone that is often carved

justified Proven to be right or correct

kingdoms Lands ruled by kings or queens

legend A story that is believed by some people to be true; its existence has not been proven

levee A wall built to prevent flooding from a river

lodestone A rock with magnetic properties

mercury A poisonous liquid silver metal

monks Religious individuals who lead simple lives and do not marry

moral Understanding right from wrong; followed a generally accepted lifestyle that shows good values

mortar A container in which a pestle is used to break down a substance

Neolithic The last period of the Stone Age, around 10,000 B.C.E.

pagoda An Asian structure with many stories and curved roofs

pestle A club-shaped tool used to break down a substance in a mortar

philosopher A person who studies ideas, such as the meaning of life, in search of truth and understanding

primary sources Materials, such as tools or written documents, created during a specific period of time

rammed earth A building material made from compressed natural materials, such as clay and soil

republic A government headed by an elected president

scholars Educated people

stern The back of something, such as a boat

submissive Without resistance; obedient

terraces Raised areas cut into a mountain or hillside on which crops are grown

terra-cotta A reddish-brown clay that is hardened by baking

trade The exchange of goods and money

Learning More

Want to learn more about ancient China? Check out these resources.

Books

Ball, Jacqueline, and Richard Levey. *Ancient China: Archaeology Unlocks the Secrets of China's Past*. National Geographic Children's Books, 2006.

Capek, Michael. *Secrets of the Terracotta Army: A Tomb of an Ancient Chinese Emperor*. Capstone Press, 2014.

Collins, Terry. *Ancient China: An Interactive History Adventure*. Capstone Press, 2012.

Culp, Jennifer. *Ancient Chinese Technology*. Rosen Young Adult, 2017.

Kopp, Megan. *Understanding Chinese Myths*. Crabtree Publishing, 2012.

Spilsbury, Louise. *Ancient China*. Capstone Press, 2016.

Websites

Travel back to ancient China on this comprehensive site from the British Museum.
www.ancientchina.co.uk/menu.html

Explore the history of China after its unification by Emperor Shihuangdi in this interactive site from the British Museum.
www.earlyimperialchina.co.uk/room.html

Watch a series of videos about the Great Wall of China from History.com.
www.history.com/topics/great-wall-of-china/videos/seven-wonders-the-great-wall

The International Dunhuang Project presents information for students about the Silk Road.
idp.bl.uk/pages/education_students.a4d

Get a close-up look at several oracle bones at the Shanghai Museum in this video from Smart History.
http://smarthistory.org/oracle-bone

Learn about and listen to bells from ancient China on the Virginia Museum of Fine Arts site.
https://vmfa.museum/interactives/beyond-the-walls/bell

INDEX

ABOUT THE AUTHOR

Kelly Spence works as a freelance author and editor for educational publishers. She holds a BA in English and Liberal Arts from Brock University, and a Certificate in Publishing from Ryerson University. She hopes to visit China someday and see the terra-cotta army of the first emperor.